5

Sight Reading for the Classical Guitar

Daily sight reading material with emphasis on interpretation, phrasing, form, etc.

by
Robert Benedict

EL 2943

What they say about "Sight Reading for the Classical Guitar"....

PROF. ELI KASSNER (Guitar Academy, Toronto): ..."Excellent, systematic and well thought out ...a very timely, necessary and useful contribution to the pedagogical material available for guitar students and teachers alike."

LIONA BOYD: "These are excellent sight reading books that will be of tremendous help to all guitar students...a most valuable contribution to classical guitar instruction."

DR. PETER DANNER (Sound Board Magazine): *"Sight Reading for the Classical Guitar* fills a void in the literature that has remained empty for far too long. The logical sequence of these pieces has been thought out with admireable care. Brief, yet complete; instructional, yet never patronizing; these short musical pieces will lead the student towards one of the greatest gifts any musician can ask for: the gift of good sight reading."

NORBERT KRAFT (Royal Conservatory of Music, University of Toronto):..."The most complete, direct system for improving the guitarist's comprehension of his instrument from a sight reading point of view."

JAMES OLDENBURG (Olsen · Oldenburg Duo): "A valuable method, both conceptually and musically."

WILLIAM FRANK (Western Board of Music): "...a welcome appearance of a much needed educational resource."

STEPHEN BOSWELL (Vancouver): "...fastidiously compiled...an invaluable teaching aid, with creative and beautiful musical material, and I give (the books) my enthusiastic support and endorsement."

MICHAEL STRUTT (University of British Columbia): "...a substantial and much needed contribution..."

I would very much like to thank DR. RON PURCELL for his encouragement, and his contributions to the study notes found throughout these volumes.
I would also like to thank many other colleagues in Canada and the United States who have encouraged and endorsed the sight reading books.

Robert Benedict

FOREWORD

This series of books for the classical guitar has been compiled to improve sight reading, an often neglected aspect of musicianship.

With the guitar, musical components (scales, chords, arpeggios, etc.) may often be played in various positions. While this is one of the reasons that the instrument produces such colorful and interesting timbres, it also contributes to the difficulties of sight reading. Inspite of, or perhaps *because* of this, it is important to develop facility in reading, recognizing the notes, as well as the bar positions in which to play them, the fingerings, the rhythmic patterns, and any markings of interpretation (dynamics, phrasing, articulation, etc.).

These books provide an orderly and systematic approach to the study of sight reading, based upon standards for sight reading for the classical guitar found in respected schools around the world. Preceding this volume are Levels One to Three, and it is recommended that these are carefully studied before progressing to Levels Four and Five.

Although the repertoire for students at Levels Four and Five is generally written in the lower positions, it is very important to develop both reading and playing in upper positions. For this purpose, a supplement of position-playing examples has been included at the end of each level.

The compositions used for sight reading here are original, written in classical and more modern styles, and they exemplify a variety of rhythmic and melodic, contrapuntal and harmonic possibilites. Throughout the levels I have offered some suggestions, both within the pieces and as footnotes, to help with one's approach to sight reading. Only a minimal amount of fingering has been added to the music, to encourage the reading of the notes themselves.

The reward for proficient sight reading will be found in the vast repertoire of beautiful music that one can then appreciate in a musical career.

Robert Benedict
Royal Conservatory of Music,
University of Toronto.

TABLE OF CONTENTS

NOTES TO THE TEACHER

This work is designed for grade school or university level in either private tutoring or class instruction, and is intended to be used by guitar students on a daily basis. The main goals of *Sight Reading for Classical Guitar* (Levels One to Three) were:

1. To prepare the beginning student in his third or fourth week of lessons to sight read material equivalent in difficulty to lesson repertoire and technical proficiency, and

2. To improve reading in the student who has already started guitar and has attained a technical level equivalent to first year.

This volume, containing Levels Four and Five, will continue the study of sight reading, providing material suitable for more advanced students. Both books can be used to establish a reading level for students entering a new environment of guitar instruction, whether it be private tuition or class lessons.

The reading level of a student should not be more than one to two steps behind their technical ability. This goal is attained through careful scrutiny by the teacher in the progression of material given to the student throughout his studies. You, the teacher, should ask the following questions when presenting new material: Why am I giving the student this study or piece? Does it follow logically what the student has learned? And, is the student ready for this repertoire? The degree to which the teacher is prepared to answer the questions demonstrates the degree of responsibility to his/her students. That is the ultimate basis of any teacher's reputation.

Dr. Ron Purcell
California State University,
Northridge.

LEVEL 4

Before Playing carefully look at the **Key Signature** and the **Time Signature.**

Look at the complete line of music before beginning to play.
Play slowly, and read ahead.
When more difficult rhythms occur (sixteenths, triplets, dotted eighths, etc.), clap or play on an open string the rhythm alone. Then begin to play the exercise.

In single-line melodies, use combinations of p, i, m, and a which are most natural and produce the nicest tone.

Use the left hand fingerings which are most convenient in order to play the passage at sight. Read ahead and prepare for sequences.

Think of the notes found in the scale indicated by the key signature (second position).
Giocoso

Sequences using tenths, similar to the following, are very common.

Read the rhythm of both parts, rests and notes.

Always sight read in a musical and convincing way,
using dynamics and shaping the phrases.

Before Playing carefully look at the **Key Signature** and the **Time Signature.**

Read slowly, and remember - one flat.

The role of each part is exchanged.

Play the triplet group and feel it continue through the following quarter note.

Feel the drumlike pulse of the triplets.

Before Playing carefully look at the **Key Signature** and the **Time Signature.**

Feel two strong beats in each measure.

Feel the quarter-note pulse within the varying rhythms of the melody.

Imagine the sound of the chromatic bass part before beginning to play.

Listen carefully to your performance of each sight reading exercise.
Hear the problems that you are having and make an effort to improve
in these areas (left hand, right hand, phrasing, etc.).

4

Before Playing carefully look at the **Key Signature** and the **Time Signature.**

Learn to recognize these common four-note chord patterns. Play slowly.

19

Mesto

20

In two-part counterpoint, there is a natural tendency to listen to the more active part; try to hear the less active voice as well.

21

Placidamente

22

legato

Before Playing carefully look at the **Key Signature** and the **Time Signature**.

This is a typical classical staccato accompaniment. Before you play, try to imagine the rhythmic effect of a pizzicato string orchestra! (See "stopped basses," bottom of page 35.)

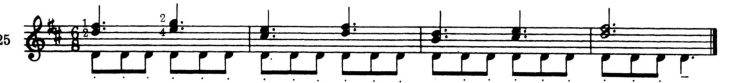

While playing the first four quarter notes, feel the sixteenth note rhythm. Play slowly.

Common dotted rhythms can be made to sound more lively and light,
by making the dotted note longer and the following note shorter.

Before Playing carefully look at the **Key Signature** and the **Time Signature.**

By reading ahead, you can recognize the broken chords and the most suitable fingerings.

Read ahead.

Notice the descending scales in both parts (relative major and minor).

FORM: A *canon* occurs when a melody begins in one part and, as it continues, is imitated in another part.
Before beginning to play, notice the imitation in the bass of the upper melody.

Before Playing carefully look at the **Key Signature** and the **Time Signature**.

FORM: A *chorale* is a melody or tune that comes from the sacred hymn literature, or that is to be played like a sacred tune.
Read the fingerings as well as the notes and rhythms.

Very slowly and legato, as a Chorale

The interval of a fourth is used here, harmonically and melodically.

Think of the sight reading exercises as little performances
in themselves. Prepare for cadences with ritards; use dynamics
and varying articulations to give colour to your playing.

Before Playing carefully look at the **Key Signature** and the **Time Signature.**

Think of the chords as being joined by the melodic fragments.

Before Playing carefully look at the **Key Signature** and the **Time Signature.**

Name the notes which are sharp before beginning to play. Think of all the notes in the scale.

Let the indicated fingerings facilitate the playing of a piece.

Read ahead.

Before you play, feel the rhythmic groups *within* a bar
(♩♩♩ or ♩.♪ or ♪♫ , etc.). Then feel how they combine with other
groups to make up the rhythm of the phrase.

Before Playing carefully look at the **Key Signature** and the **Time Signature.**

Feel the quarter-note pulse and the triplets within.

Learn to recognize the common chord patterns, especially in the more common keys for the guitar.

Play musically. Approach a piece in the character indicated by the expression marking.

Before Playing carefully look at the **Key Signature** and the **Time Signature.**

Look at the complete line of music before beginning to play. See the arpeggio patterns as a group, and read ahead to the next bar.

Play gracefully, with a feeling of one beat per bar.

Varying articulation enhances a piece and gives it character. (See "stopped basses", bottom page 35.)

Sight read as often as possible, choosing easier pieces
(approximately two levels lower than your current technical
level). Play with expression, shaping phrases and using dynamics.

12

Before Playing carefully look at the **Key Signature** and the **Time Signature.**

Read the bar indications first; the other fingerings will follow.

Read carefully the fingerings in this little piece. Also, recognize the sequential patterns.

* bar with the index finger two out of six strings at the first position.

Before Playing carefully look at the **Key Signature** and the **Time Signature.**

Feel the lilting rhythm of this piece before you begin to play.

Melodies which are chromatic should be read very slowly.

Feel the character of the piece before playing. Much of
your ability to sight read depends upon your emotional
interpretation and approach.

14

Before playing, look carefully through the complete line of music.
Notice how the moving triplets are alternated between the parts.

Aim for a performance *without* mistakes.

Before Playing carefully look at the **Key Signature** and the **Time Signature.**

"Play" the rests (by stopping the notes) to achieve the true character of the piece.

Proper fingering of one bar of music will often
set up the playing of the following bar or phrase.

POSITION-PLAYING SUPPLEMENT

This supplement is a continuation of the study of the second, third, and fifth positions. In Level Three of *Sight Reading for the Classical Guitar*, only the notes found on the first three strings in these positions were used. Here, however, the second and fifth positions will be extended to include the notes found on all six strings.

THE FIFTH POSITION

The fifth position is the most often used upper position, because music written in the common keys of C major and A minor is easily played here. More than two octaves of the natural notes fall into this position. In this way it is to a degree similar to the first position. Other keys, that require sharps of flats, also fall easily into the fifth position, and some of these will be used in this supplement.

Method of Study: For each position, study each note in Diagram A, naming it out loud, and then locate and play the note on the fingerboard, with the help of Diagram B. Treat each note as a separate sight reading exercise.

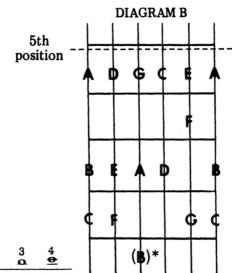

DIAGRAM B
5th position

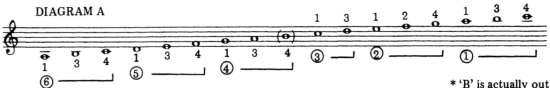

DIAGRAM A

* 'B' is actually out of the fifth position, but can be played with a stretch of the fourth finger.

THE SECOND POSITION

These are the most common notes which are played in the second position. At a glance it can be seen that these are the notes found in the scales of D major and B minor.

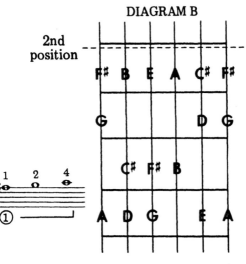

DIAGRAM B
2nd position

DIAGRAM A

THE THIRD POSITION

In this supplement, the sight reading exercises played in the third position will require only the notes found on the first three strings.

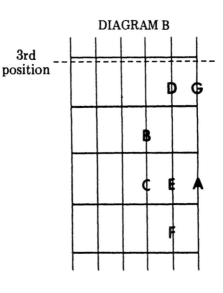

DIAGRAM B
3rd position

DIAGRAM A

"pos." (position) indicates the position in
which the left hand is to play the exercise.

After a thorough study of page 16, slowly play the following melodic fragments (examples 70 to 74)
in the positions indicated.

Examples 75 to 82 are all to be played in the fifth position. Bass notes are to be played open.

FIFTH POSITION (continued)

Look at all the natural notes found on the fingerboard in the third position on the first three strings (see page 16), and study them carefully before beginning to play.

Examples 85 to 91 can be played in more than one position.
Think of the notes in each position before beginning to play.

20

HARMONIC INTERVALS in the FIRST and FIFTH POSITIONS

Harmonic intervals have been included here to further our study of the fifth position. Each interval should be treated as a separate exercise in sight reading. First, play the interval in the first position. Name the two notes out loud, and then transpose and play them in the fifth position. Take time to study the finger patterns of each interval.

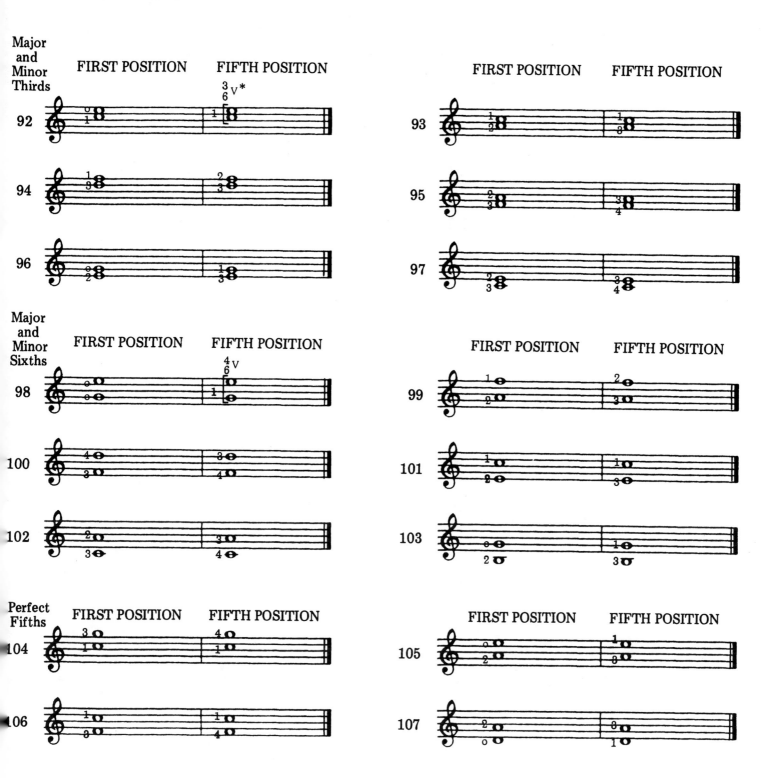

* Bar, with index finger, three of six strings at the fifth fret

RHYTHMS

Clap, or play on an open string, the following rhythmic patterns, *as well as the rhythms of the preceding pieces*, counting out loud.

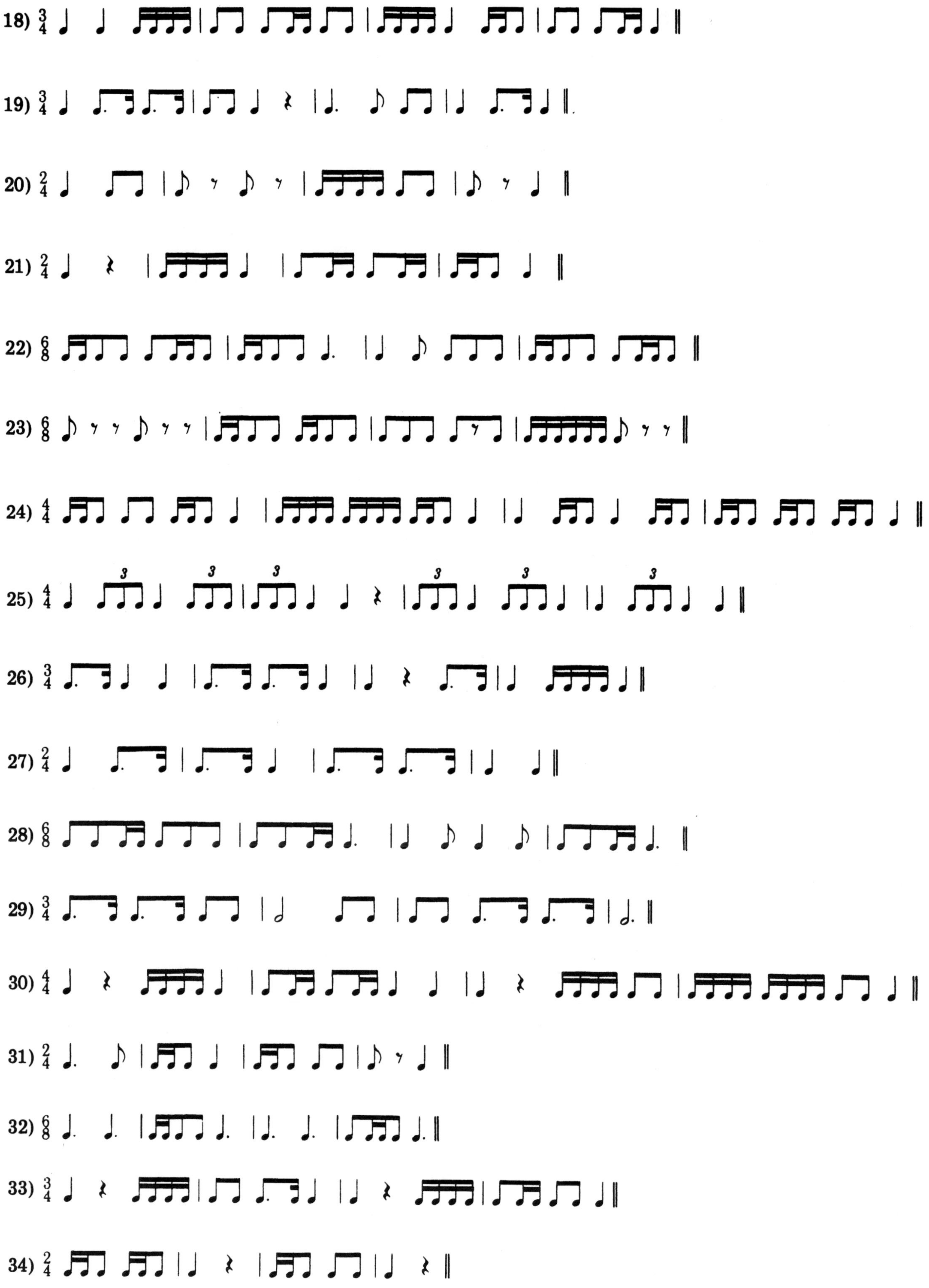
18)
19)
20)
21)
22)
23)
24)
25)
26)
27)
28)
29)
30)
31)
32)
33)
34)

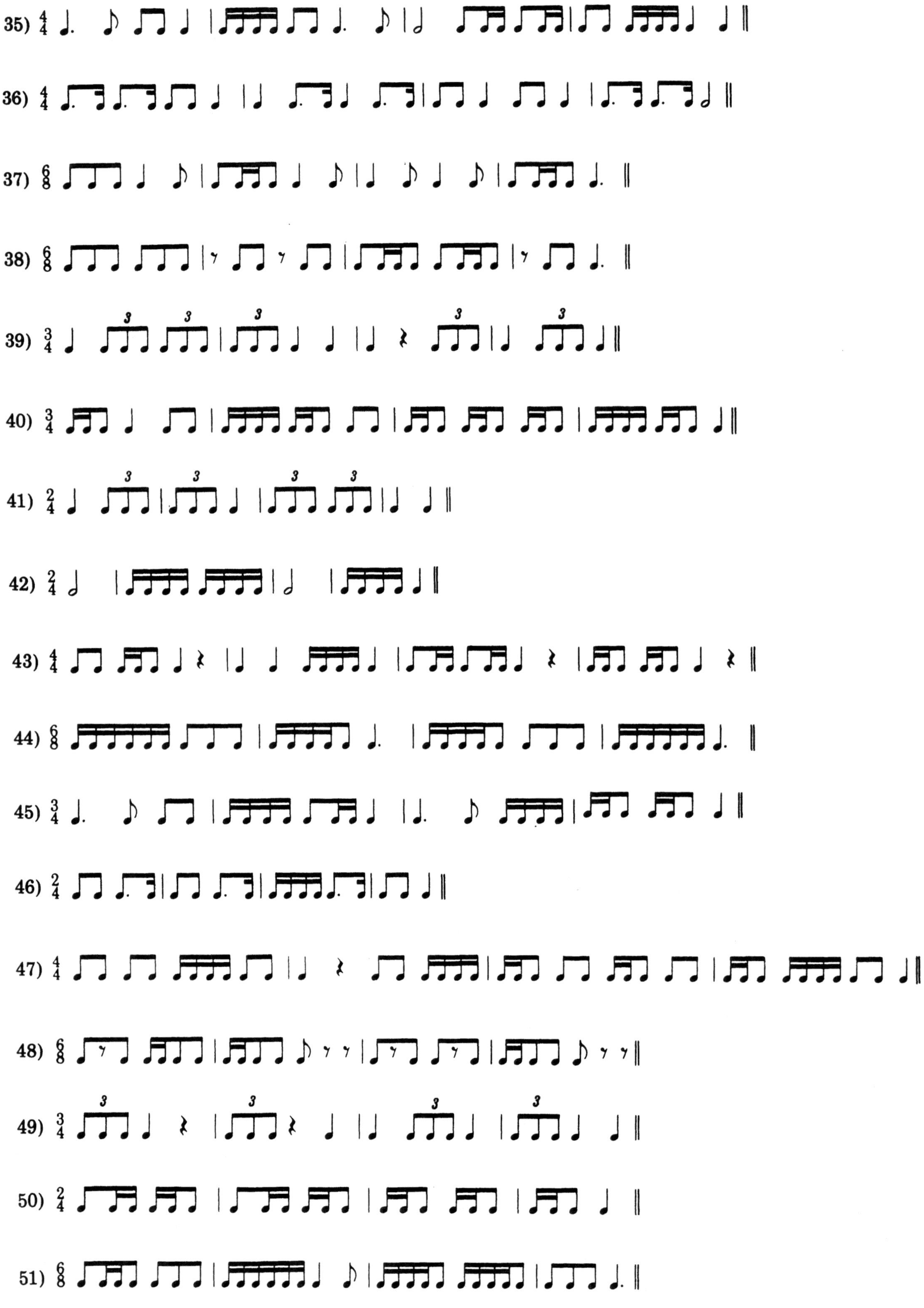
35) 4/4
36) 4/4
37) 6/8
38) 6/8
39) 3/4
40) 3/4
41) 2/4
42) 2/4
43) 4/4
44) 6/8
45) 3/4
46) 2/4
47) 4/4
48) 6/8
49) 3/4
50) 2/4
51) 6/8

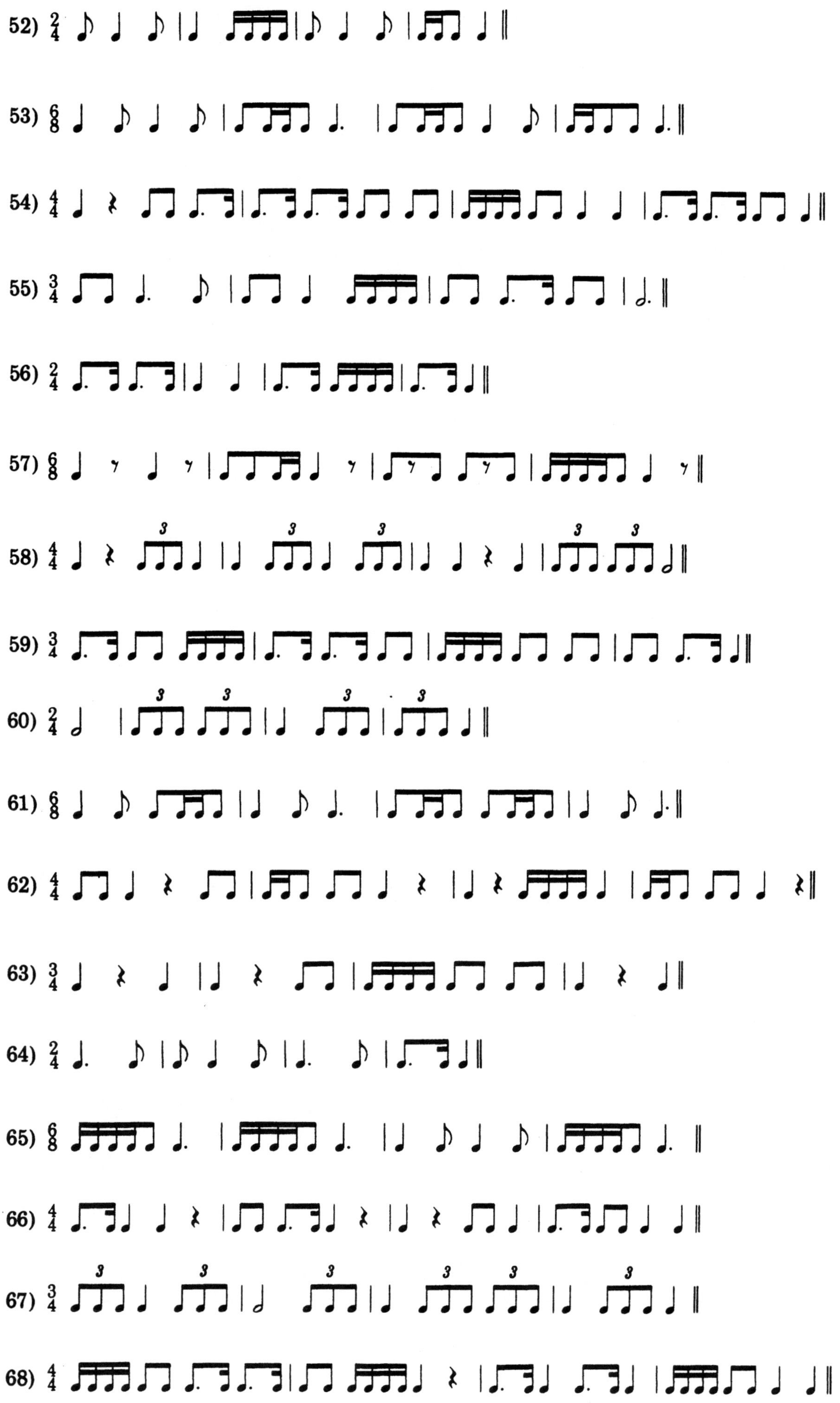
52)
53)
54)
55)
56)
57)
58)
59)
60)
61)
62)
63)
64)
65)
66)
67)
68)

LEVEL 5

Before Playing carefully look at the **Key Signature** and the **Time Signature**.

Look at the complete line of music before beginning to play.
Play slowly, and read ahead.
When more difficult rhythms occur, clap or play on an open string the rhythm alone. Then begin to play the exercise.

While playing the first four quarter notes, feel the sixteenth note rhythm.

At a quick glance, notice that all the intervals are the same.

Religioso

Identify the common chords in a key, recognizing the chord patterns (scale of D major).

Make an effort to play from the beginning to the end of
a line without stopping. Play slowly and musically.

Before Playing carefully look at the **Key Signature** and the **Time Signature.**

In two-part counterpoint, one often tends to listen to the more active part; try to hear the less active voice as well.

Play musically. Approach a piece in the character indicated by the expression marking.

Avoid the tendency to rush when playing slurred passages.

Keep the quarter-note pulse steady, as you shift from triplets to eighth notes.

See "stopped basses", bottom page 35.

The beauty of individual melodies is enhanced when they are combined with each other to provide counterpoint.

28

Before Playing carefully look at the **Key Signature** and the **Time Signature.**

ORNAMENTS are used to embellish or decorate a melodic line. One type of ornamentation, the *trill*, is used most often at a cadence. Look carefully at ornaments before playing. Feel how they will be naturally incorporated into the piece.

Read through the complete line of music before beginning to play. The stopped basses (all A's) establish the character of the piece. (See "stopped basses", bottom page 35.)

Before Playing carefully look at the **Key Signature** and the **Time Signature.**

Name the sharps before you begin. Think of the scale notes in the key.

Try to feel the character of a piece by reading it through before you
begin to play. Enhance the character with various techniques
(arpeggiated chords, different articulations and tone colours, etc.).

Before Playing carefully look at the **Key Signature** and the **Time Signature.**

This fragment uses *lower mordents* which, unlike trills, are more often found throughout a melodic line.
Ornaments should sound relaxed and improvised. Play very slowly.

Look at the complete line of music before beginning to play. Avoid watching the repeated arpeggio notes; look for the notes which are changing. Read ahead.

E major.

Before Playing carefully look at the **Key Signature** and the **Time Signature.**

At a quick glance, notice a pedal in the upper part - read ahead on the lower part.

Play musically. Approach a piece in the character indicated by the expression marking.

Imaginatively

Concentrate on the moving part.

Try to dynamically balance pieces written in
two parts. Listen carefully to your playing.

32

Before Playing carefully look at the **Key Signature** and the **Time Signature.**

Before playing this little piece, feel the rhythmic accompaniment parts and imagine the legato melody. Feel two strong beats per measure.

Before Playing carefully look at the **Key Signature** and the **Time Signature.**

Look through the complete piece. Before beginning to play, prepare in your mind the performance of the ornaments. Notice the *upper mordents* at the beginning of the line.

Play as legato as possible, *slowly,* and in a chorale, or church-like style.

Look for the little things that are frequently giving you
problems (barring, ornaments, accidentals, etc.). Work on
these areas to improve your playing and reading. Play slowly.

34

Before Playing carefully look at the **Key Signature** and the **Time Signature**.

String indications and fingerings will help with the reading.

Look for sequences. Prepare for the dotted rhythm before you begin.

See "stopped basses", bottom page 35.

Before Playing carefully look at the **Key Signature** and the **Time Signature.**

Read the bar indications first; the other fingerings will follow.

Notice the three separate parts or voices.

The nature of this piece is found in the contrasting staccato and legato notes of the bass part. Read slowly.

By studying staccato playing with the thumb, learn to control the bass parts. Almost any piece can be used as an exercise to learn to stop basses. Learn to avoid harmonic 4ths and 5ths, which occur when the strings continue to vibrate. With this, sight reading will improve because the overall performance will always be better.

36

Before Playing carefully look at the **Key Signature** and the **Time Signature.**

In single-line pieces, read as far ahead as possible.

"Play" the rests by stopping the chords.

Thoughtfully

Before Playing carefully look at the **Key Signature** and the **Time Signature.**

Play very slowly and freely. Maintain the quarter note pulse.

The offbeat accents in the accompaniment provide the characteristic feel of this piece.

The more difficult a piece appears at first sight,
the more carefully it should be approached.

Before Playing carefully look at the **Key Signature** and the **Time Signature**.

Look through the complete piece before beginning to play. Clap and feel the rhythm.

Notice the right hand finger pattern which is established in the first measure.

It is most important to understand the musical nature of a piece
before beginning to play. If no expression marking is indicated,
study the piece a little before starting. Is it rhythmic,
contrapuntal, a melody with accompaniment? etc.

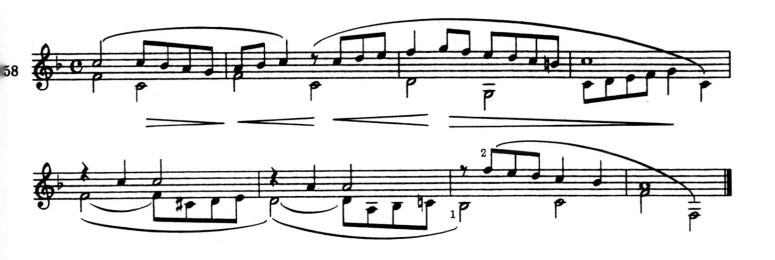

40

Before Playing carefully look at the **Key Signature** and the **Time Signature.**

Listen for sequences.
Teneramente

Here we have a strong feeling of two beats to a measure. Practise clapping the shift from triplets to (2) eighth notes.

Keep the rhythm of the quarter notes steady as the time signature changes.

Sight read as though you were performing.
Play convincingly and sensitively.

POSITION-PLAYING SUPPLEMENT

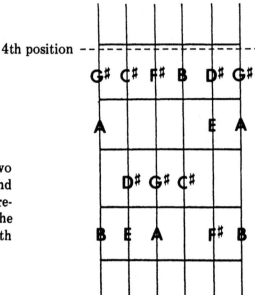

DIAGRAM B

THE FOURTH POSITION

At a quick glance it may be seen that there are more than two octaves of notes from the keys of E major and C♯ minor found here. Melodies, chords, fragments, etc. from these keys are therefore often played in this position. We will frequently find the open bass E and open subdominant A used in conjunction with the fourth position.

DIAGRAM A

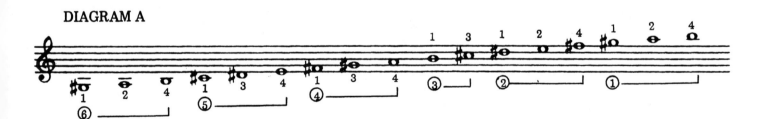

Method of Study: Play each note in Diagram A, naming it out loud, and then locate and play the note on the fingerboard, with the help of Diagram B. Treat each note as a separate sight reading exercise.

The second, third, and fifth positions are reviewed again in Level Five; read over page 16 in Level Four to be thoroughly familiar with the notes. In this supplement, some less common keys have been included, which fall easily into these positions. For example, fifth position - E♭ major, C minor, B♭ major, G minor, etc.

"pos." (position) indicates the position in
which the left hand is to play the exercise.

Play the following melodic fragments (examples 64 to 67) in the positions indicated.

FIRST AND FIFTH POSITIONS

Play each of the following scales and melodic fragments (examples 68 to 75) in the *first position, and then in the fifth position.* Before beginning to play, look at the key signature; try to hear the tonality (major or minor), and think of the notes which make up the scale. Use a fifth position bar if necessary.

* The fourth finger expands or reaches for the 'B'.
The left hand itself should remain in the fifth position.

FIRST AND FIFTH POSITIONS (cont'd)

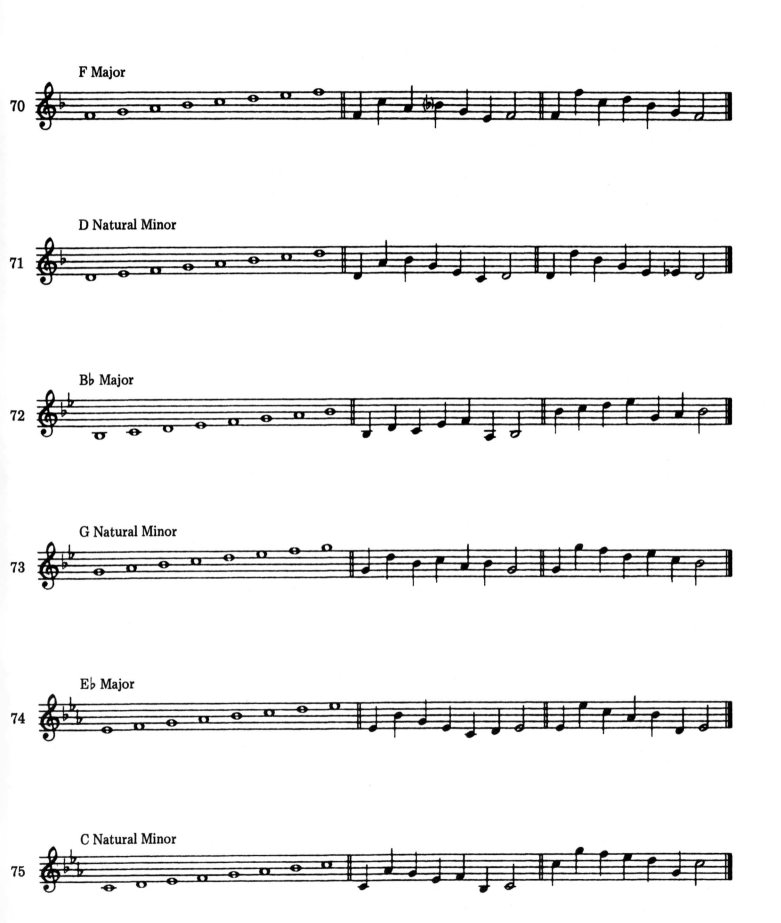

SECOND POSITION

Play each of the following scales and melodic fragments (examples 76 to 83) in *the second position* only. Before beginning to play, look at the key signature; try to hear the tonality (major or minor), and think of the notes which make up the scale. Use a second position bar if necessary.

C Major

2nd pos.   2   4   1   2   4   1   3   4   2   1   4

A Natural Minor

G Major

E Natural Minor

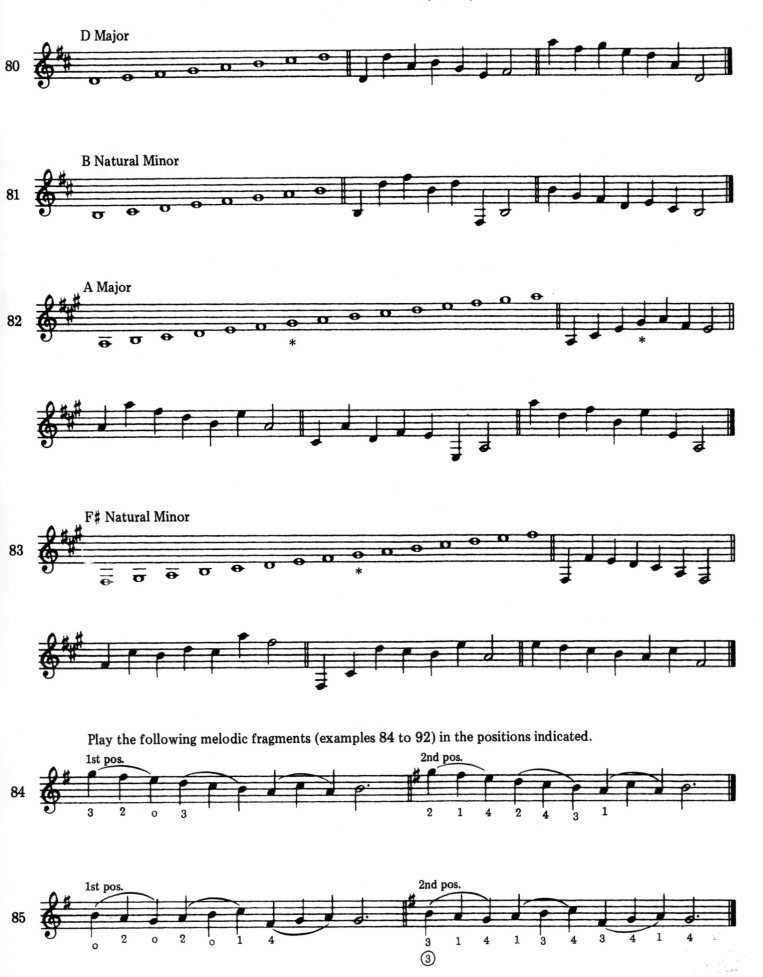

Play the following melodic fragments (examples 84 to 92) in the positions indicated.

* Keep the left hand over the second position.

Use a full bar $\left(\substack{6\\6}\right)$ in the fifth position.

93

Use a half bar $\left(\substack{3\\6}\right)$ in the fourth position.

94

Examples 95 and 96 use two different bar positions, with an open string accompaniment.

95

96

Examples 97 to 102 can be played in more than one position.
Think of the notes in each position before beginning to play.

1st pos.

97
a)

2nd pos.

b)

5th pos.

c)

48

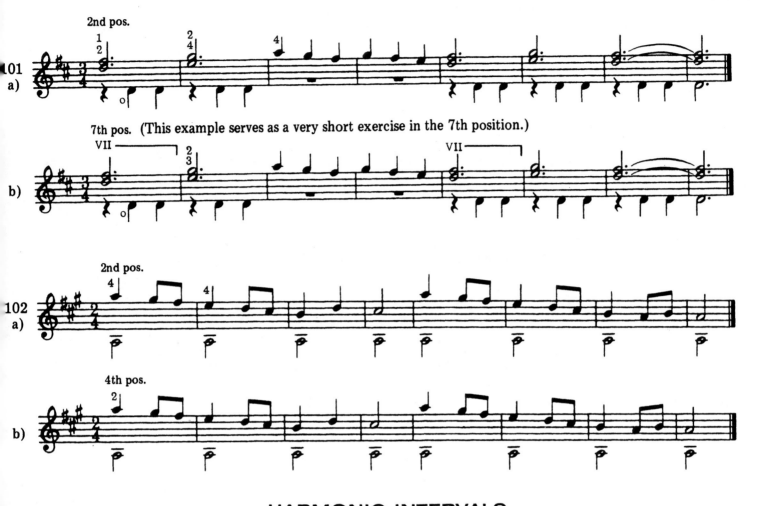

HARMONIC INTERVALS

Each interval should be treated as a separate exercise in sight reading. First, play the interval in the first position. Name the two notes out loud, and then transpose and play them in the upper position. Take time to study the finger patterns of each interval.

FIRST AND FIFTH POSITIONS

Play the following intervals (examples 103 to 112) in the *first and fifth positions*. Use bars where necessary.
Examples 103 to 107 use only notes which are natural (without accidentals) and found easily in the fifth position.

FIRST AND FIFTH POSITIONS (cont'd)

Perfect Octaves

106

Major and Minor Tenths

107

Examples 108 to 112 include accidentals. Name the two notes out loud before transposing them into the fifth position.

Major and Minor Thirds

108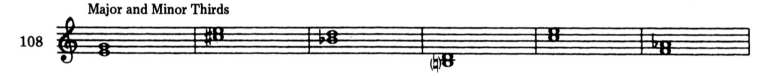

Perfect Fifths

109

FIRST AND FIFTH POSITIONS (cont'd)

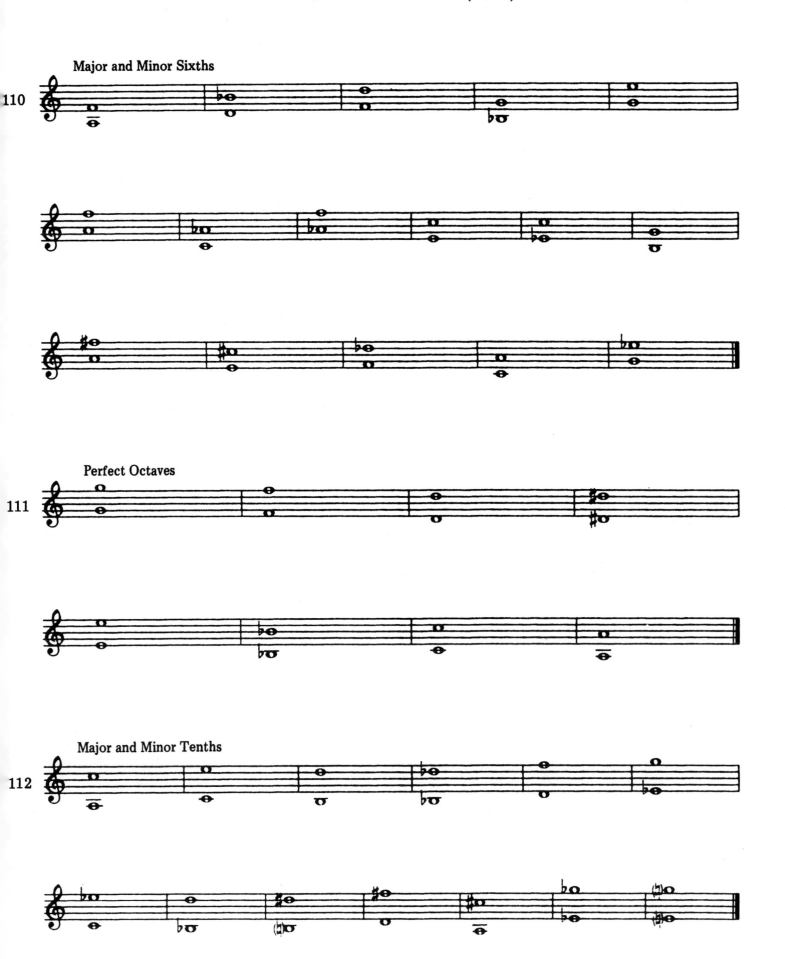

Play the following fragments in the first position, and then in the fifth position. Use bars where necessary.

113

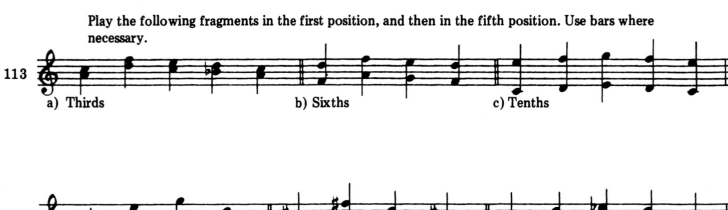

a) Thirds   b) Sixths   c) Tenths

d) Fifths   e) Tenths   f) Octaves

g) Sixths   h) Octaves   i) Thirds

j) Tenths   k) Fifths   l) Sixths

Play the following triads in the first *and* fifth positions.

114

C Major (first inversion)   C Major (second inversion)   F Major   F Minor   A Major   A Minor   D Minor (second inversion)

115

SECOND POSITION

Play the following intervals (examples 116 to 120) in *the second position* only. Some open notes may be used. Use bars where necessary.

Major and Minor Thirds

Major and Minor Sixths

SECOND POSITION (cont'd)

Major and Minor Sixths (cont'd)

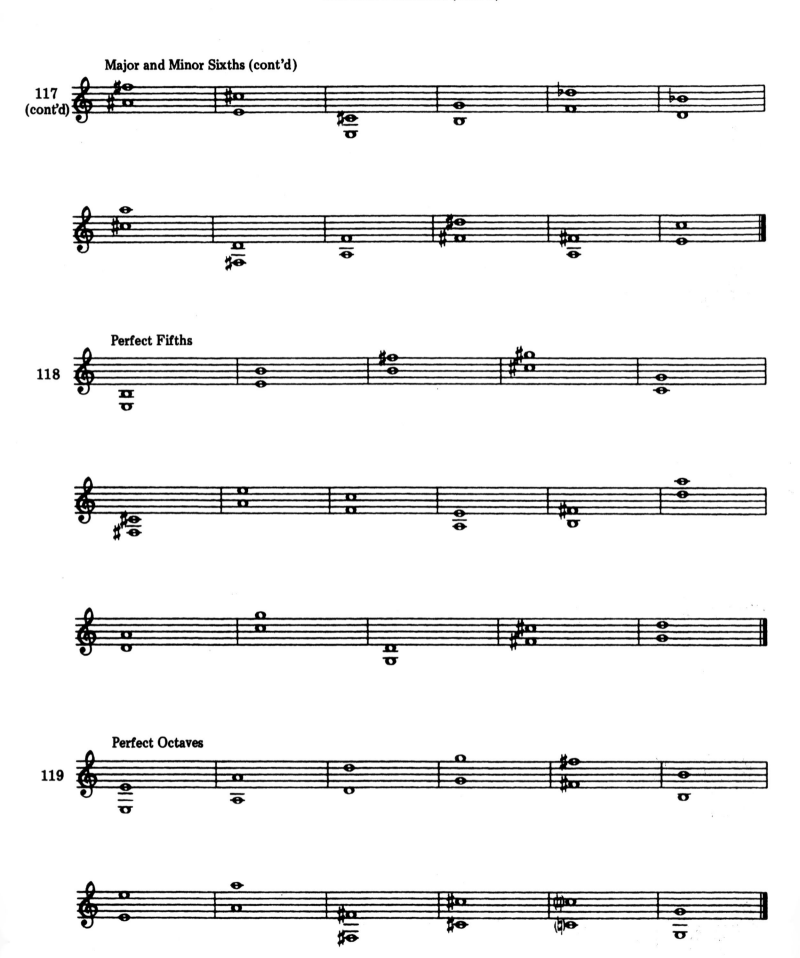

SECOND POSITION (cont'd)

Major and Minor Tenths

Play the following fragments in the second position. Use bars where necessary.

a) Thirds   b) Fifths

c) Octaves   d) Sixths   e) Thirds

f) Sixths   g) Tenths

h) Fifths   i) Tenths   j) Octaves

RHYTHMS

Clap or play on an open string, the following rhythmic patterns, *as well as the rhythms of the preceding pieces,* counting out loud.

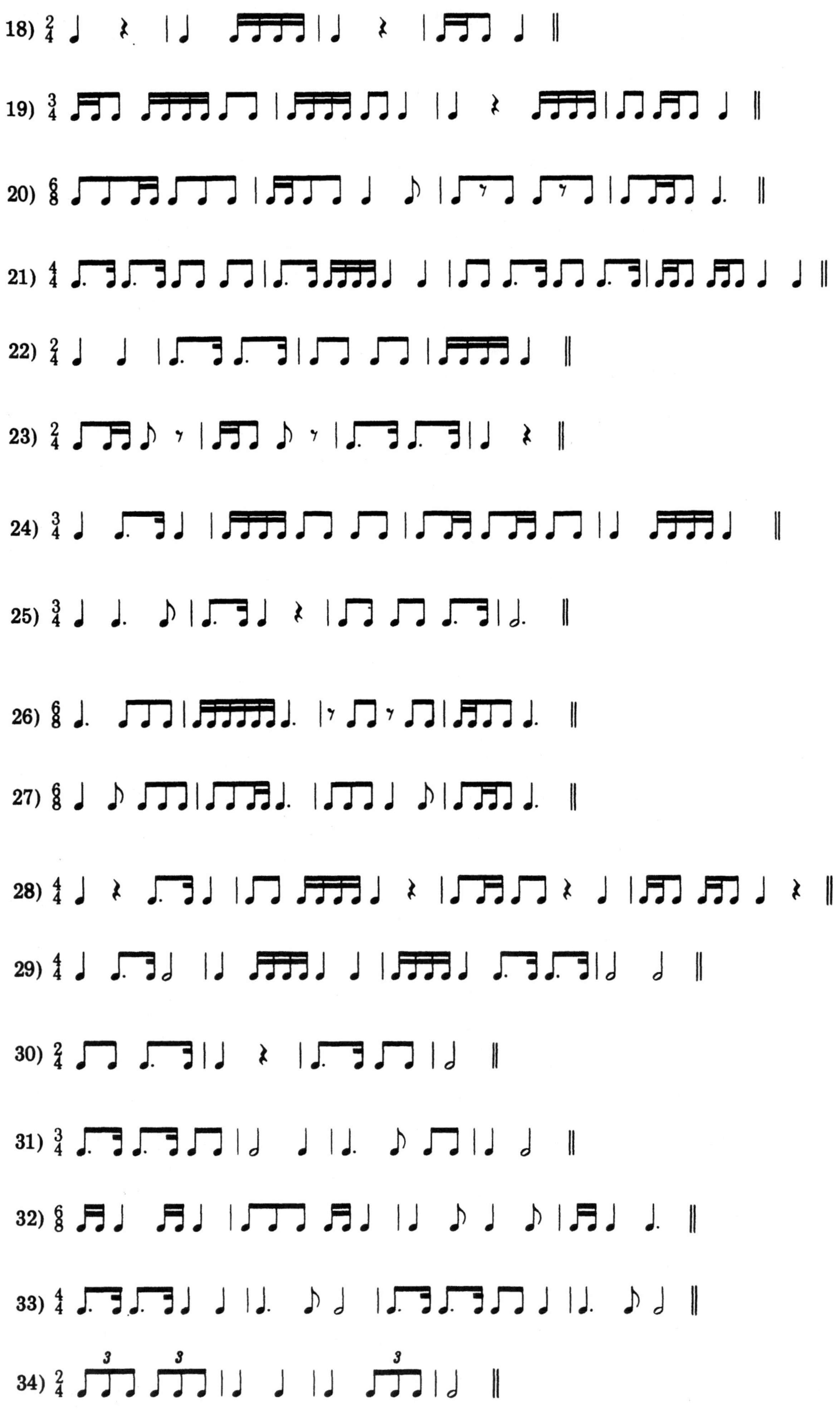
18)
19)
20)
21)
22)
23)
24)
25)
26)
27)
28)
29)
30)
31)
32)
33)
34)

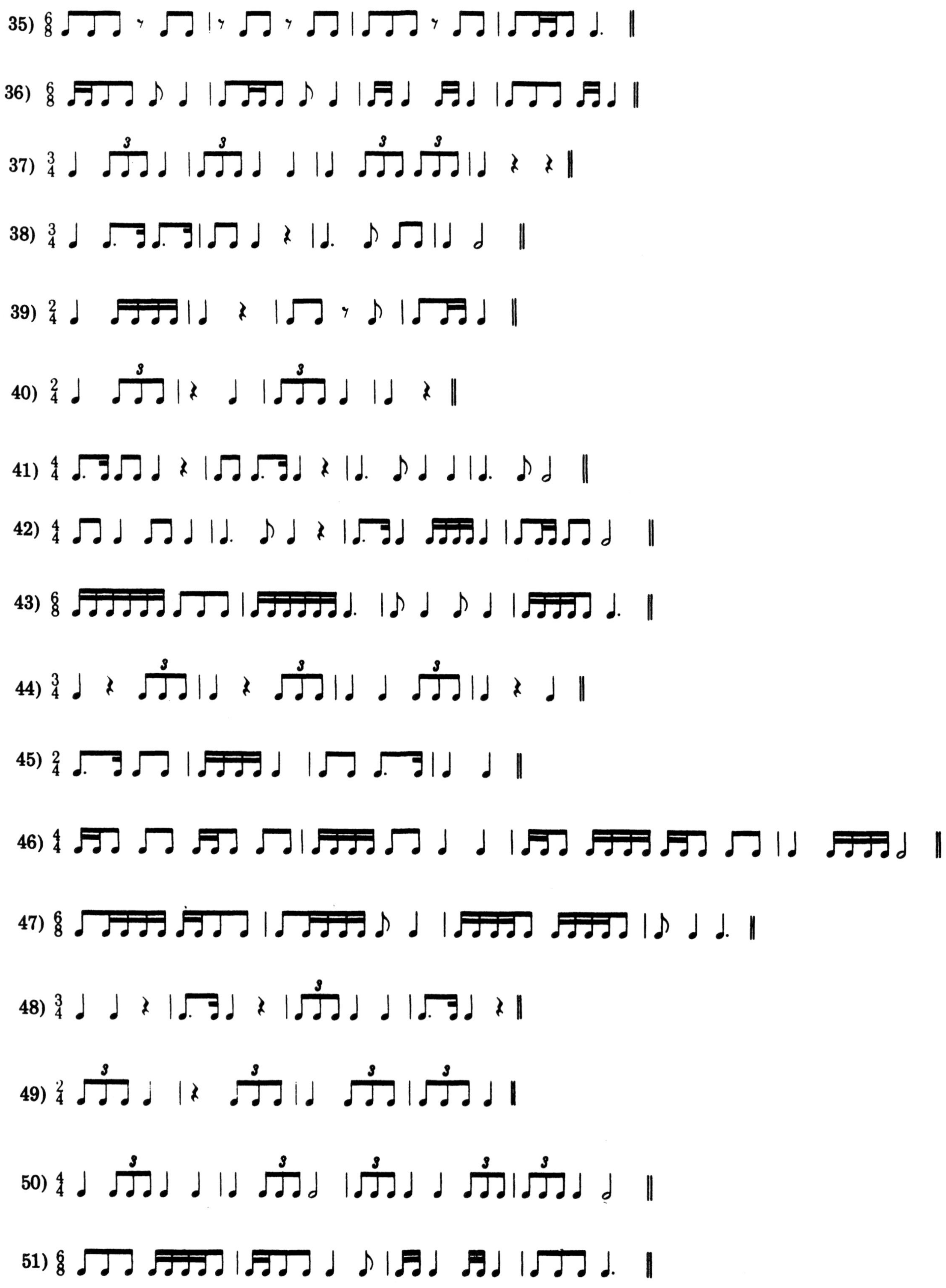
35)
36)
37)
38)
39)
40)
41)
42)
43)
44)
45)
46)
47)
48)
49)
50)
51)

52) 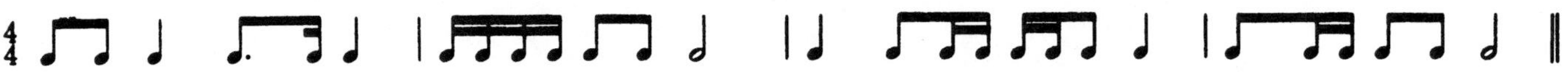

53) 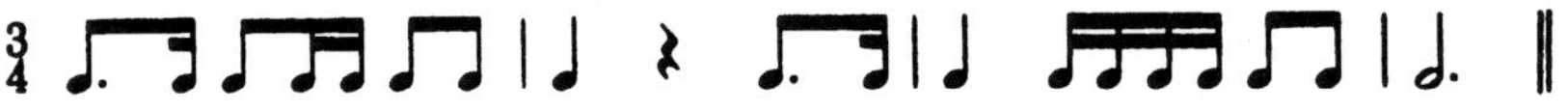

54) 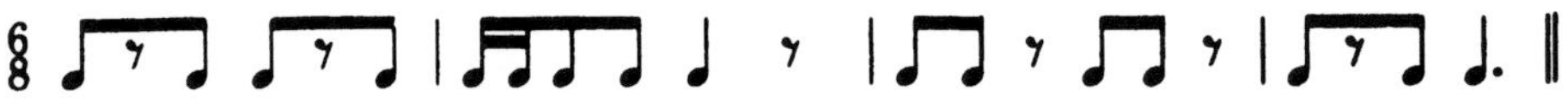

55) 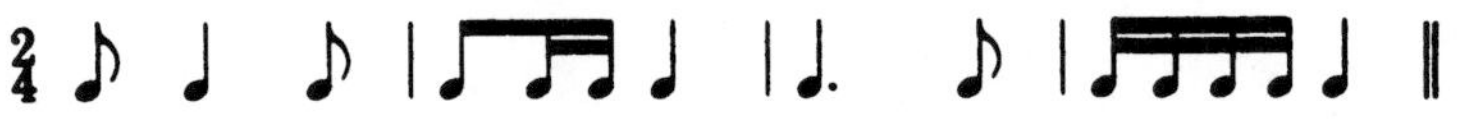

56) 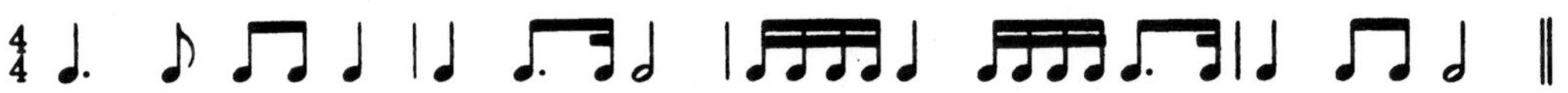

57) 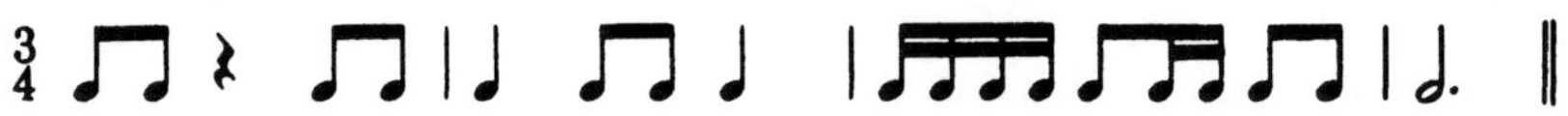

58) 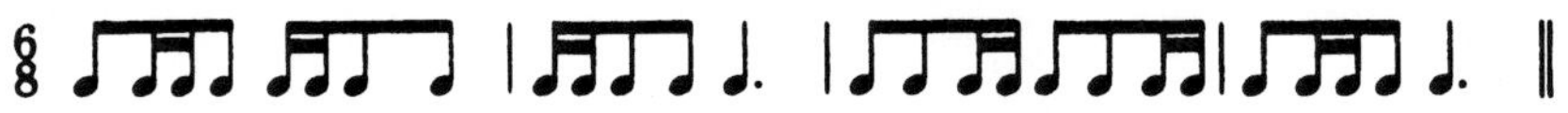

59) 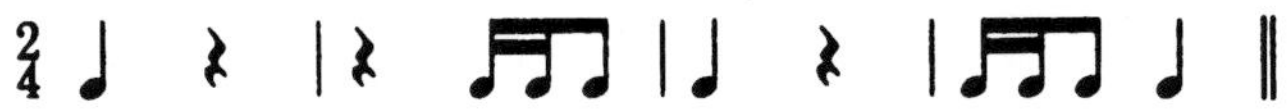

60) 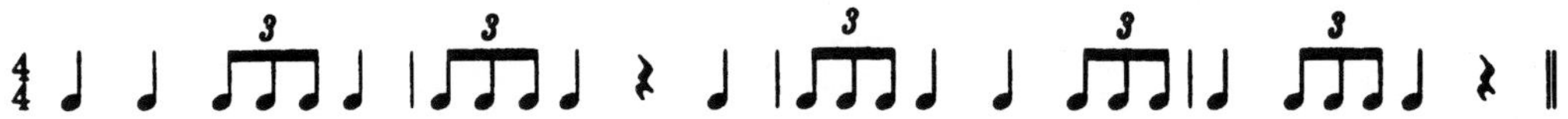

61) 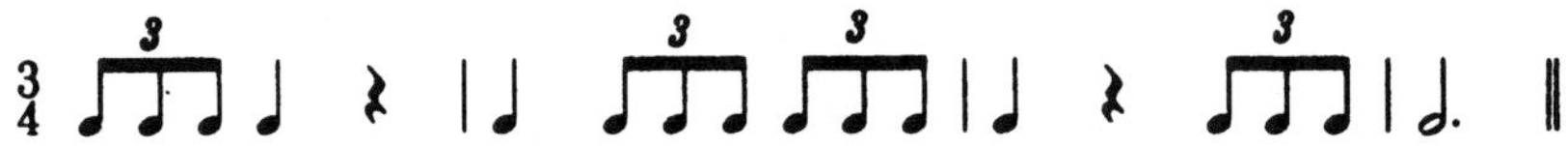

62) 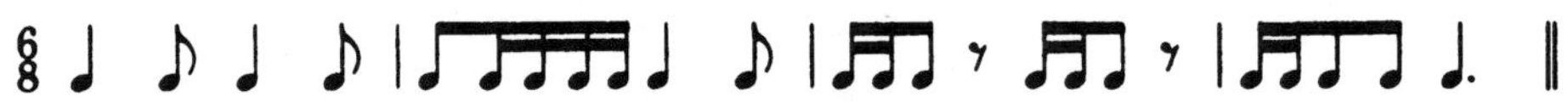

63) 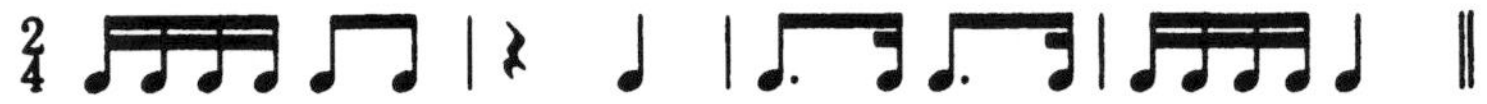

64) 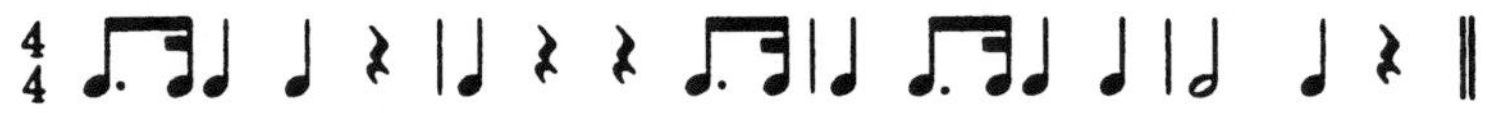

65) 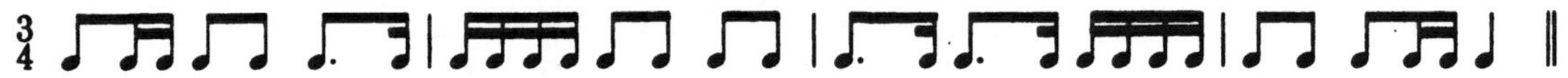

66) 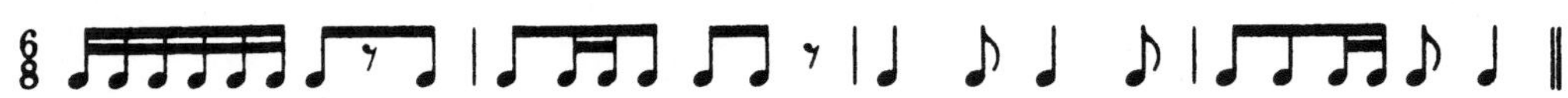

67) 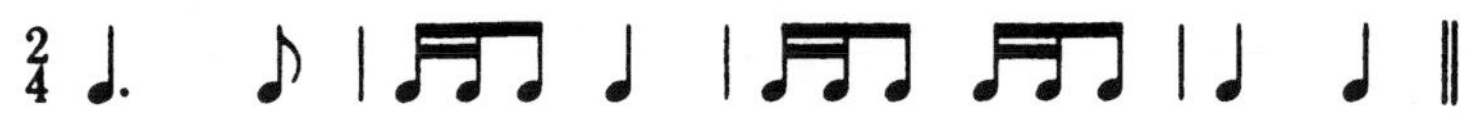

68) 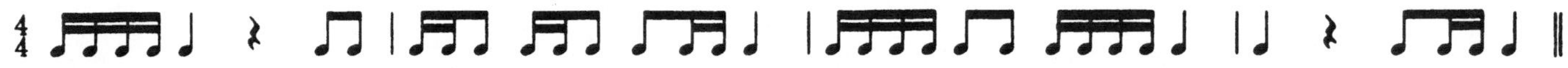

EXPRESSION MARKINGS

The following is a short list of some of the more common Italian expression markings, many of which have been included in this book.

agitato	excited
animato	with spirit
cantabile	in a singing style
con moto	with motion
con spirito	with spirit
delicato	delicately
dolce	sweetly
dolente	with sorrow
espressivo	with expression
facilmente	easily, without strain
furioso	furiously
giocoso	playfully
grandioso	grandly
grazioso	gracefully
maestoso	majestically, dignified
marcato	emphasized
mesto	sadly
pesante	heavily
piacevole	pleasing, agreeable
placidamente	peacefully
religioso	religiously, devotedly
scherzando	playfully
semplice	simply
solenne	solemnly
sostenuto	sustained
tempo rubato	in 'robbed' time, flexibility and freedom with the phrasing
teneramente	tenderly
tranquillo	calmly, quietly
vivace	with life